BEGIN ONE WAY

A CHILDREN'S BOOK OF ROAD SIGNS

By Ioana Stoian

Illustrated by Sophia Vincent Guy

Published in 2022 by Busy Hands Books
busyhandsbooks.com

Text copyright ©2022 Ioana Stoian
Illustrations copyright ©2022 Sophia Vincent Guy

A catalogue record for this book is available from the British Library.

ISBN 978-0-9576192-2-7

Printed and bound in USA

For curious children everywhere.

There's so much to see when we go for a walk;
we can hold someone's hand, we can have a nice talk.
We can look all around and play games like "I spy";
we can watch all the cars and the trucks driving by.

But one of my favorite things we can do
is to look for road signs — and we find quite a few!
The words and the pictures are part of a code
that keeps us all safe when we're out near a road.
Come listen, I'll tell you what some of them mean,
you may even find ones that you haven't seen!

Let's walk down to one of my favorite places.
We'll find books by the hundreds and friendly faces.

BEGIN ONE WAY is the first sign we meet
as it stands rather tall at the top of my street
and it means that there's only one way they can go;
we're not in a car, but we'll go with the flow.

At a **RIGHT TURN ONLY,** cars can only turn right;
this sign spells it out here, in black and in white.

The **STOP** sign is bold and it's bright and it's clear;
we'll count all eight sides when we get nice and near.

A circle with a line right through it means 'no';
NO LEFT TURN, NO U-TURN — so, on we go!

DO NOT ENTER tells drivers they can't come on through.
On this one-way street, there's not one sign, but two!

At a **RAILROAD CROSSING,** a train might be near!
Only cross over when ALL tracks are clear!

At a **YIELD** sign, cars must slow down and give way
to the bikes, cars and trucks or to tractors with hay!

YIELD

You'll find them at **TRAFFIC CIRCLES** or a **ROUNDABOUT**
where the arrows all point to the different ways out.

A **SPEED LIMIT** sign with the number 25
shows all the cars just how fast they can drive.

A picture of a seesaw, what else could it be?
The **PLAYGROUND** sign always fills me with glee.

NIGHT PLOW ROUTE might be one you don't know,
but in Minnesota, we get lots of snow!
This sign is on roads that get plowed overnight,
and while the plows work cars must not be in sight.

Oh look: I spy green, and then yellow, and red;
I think that a **TRAFFIC LIGHT** is **UP AHEAD!**

Now these two are very important to know,

DON'T WALK means we stop.

And **WALK** means we go!

P stands for parking, but not along here.
NO PARKING makes sure that this road remains clear.

A **BIKE LANE** gives cyclists some extra protection; here, they can cycle in either direction.

ROAD WORK AHEAD what is happening here?
The road's all dug up, and construction is near.

The **DETOUR** sign shows cars how to get 'round the diggers, the workers, and that giant mound!

A **PEDESTRIAN CROSSING,** let's hold our hands tight
and turn our heads both to the left and the right.

Look, we've arrived at our destination!
The **LIBRARY** is such a special location.
Everyone's welcome to read and to play —
let's go on in, the door is this way!

Here are some road signs we just spotted on our walk, as well as a few more that you might recognize from your own outdoor adventures.

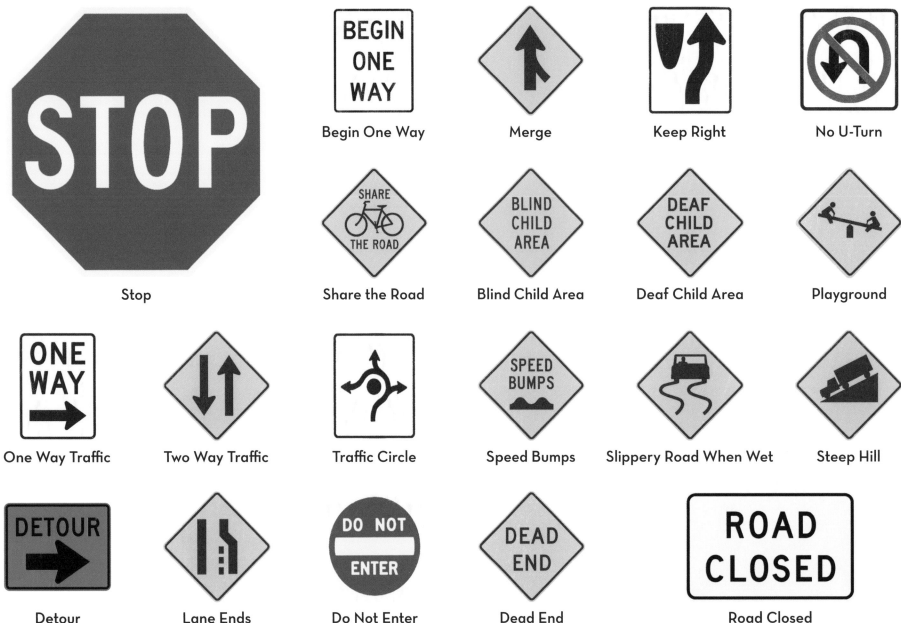

STOP
Stop

BEGIN ONE WAY
Begin One Way

Merge

Keep Right

No U-Turn

SHARE THE ROAD
Share the Road

BLIND CHILD AREA
Blind Child Area

DEAF CHILD AREA
Deaf Child Area

Playground

ONE WAY
One Way Traffic

Two Way Traffic

Traffic Circle

SPEED BUMPS
Speed Bumps

Slippery Road When Wet

Steep Hill

DETOUR
Detour

Lane Ends

DO NOT ENTER
Do Not Enter

DEAD END
Dead End

ROAD CLOSED
Road Closed

Tow Away Zone

No Left Turn

No Right Turn

Left Turn Only

Right Turn Only

Disability Parking

No Parking

No Trucks

Speed Limit

Traffic Light Ahead

Road Work Ahead

Bike Lane

Deer Crossing

Pedestrian Crossing

Rail Road Crossing

Yield

Library

Fire Station

Hospital

School Zone

Ioana Stoian lives in a bright pink house in St. Paul, Minnesota with her husband and sign-spotting son. When she's not writing books or taking walks, Ioana can be found in the kitchen baking fresh bread, digging outside in the garden, or in her favorite armchair reading about child development. And wherever she goes, a half-empty cup of tea follows.

Ioana is the author of the board book *Always be You* and this is her first picture book. You can find out more about her at: ioanastoian.com

Sophia Vincent Guy is a Canadian-born architect-turned-illustrator currently living in Israel with her husband and two children. When she's not drawing road signs from her home studio, she's usually cooking, crafting and dancing with her family.

Learn more about Sophia on her website: sophiavincentguy.com

Author's Note

This book is primarily about road signs and what they mean. As a parent, I see first-hand just how curious children are about the world they inhabit, and how eager they are to be a valued member of the community they live in. As road signs play an important role in our day to day lives, this book delivers useful information about them in an age-appropriate way. I hope it empowers children to actively and safely participate in habitual actions like crossing the road.

But, this book is also about the importance of being fully present with our children and with our surroundings. In our stress-filled and fast paced lives we can easily forget to slow down and simply breathe. Let's remember to carve out intentional time where we follow our children's pace, join them in their curiosity, and give them our undivided attention.

Happy sign spotting!